The Life Expansion Playbook
30 Days to a More Fulfilling Life

Mark Warren

CROSSBOOKS

CrossBooks™
1663 Liberty Drive
Bloomington, IN 47403
www.crossbooks.com
Phone: 1-866-879-0502

©2010 Mark Warren. All rights reserved.

No part of this book may be reproduced, stored in a retrieval system, or transmitted by any means without the written permission of the author.

First published by CrossBooks 2/25/2010

ISBN: 978-1-6150-7075-6 (sc)

Library of Congress Control Number: 2009940819

Printed in the United States of America
Bloomington, Indiana

This book is printed on acid-free paper.

Before We Begin...

Life is not about your own greatness but about _____.

Take a second to think about this incomplete sentence. How you fill in the blank directly depends on how you view the world around you. It depends on how you view culture, life, family, friends, and work. Arriving at your final decision about what you want to put in the blank space can be a difficult process. One person might discover the answer to this question after looking for the source of all his success. Another person might find the same answer while rebounding from a tragic family accident. No matter the circumstances, it's the final decision that's important.

I have been coaching for 15 years, and every year I've coached I have had a playbook. A playbook contains rules and guidelines for achieving a desired outcome. This book has a similar purpose—it can serve as a "playbook" for your life. I believe that if you'll set aside 30 days and use them to apply the challenges outlined on the pages that follow, it will guide you in deciding just how you want to fill in the blank and finish the sentence.

Why do you need a playbook? Here are some possible reasons:

1. You are dazed and confused by the variety of life choices out there.
2. You've tried a bunch of stuff, worked hard to achieve certain goals, and are dismayed by post-victory disappointment and restlessness.

3. You're curious to see if maybe you missed something. Maybe there's something really cool right over the horizon you haven't yet considered.
4. Perhaps when you looked in the bathroom mirror this morning you saw a half-dead stranger in a terrible hurry to go somewhere you didn't really want to go.
5. You have a nagging sense that there must be more to life than what we have come up with so far.
6. As David Byrne from the Talking Heads sang in his song "Stop Making Sense," your life doesn't make sense and you are worn out from pretending to be doing something really important.

The playbook gives coaches a chance to look at their team's issues, problems, training, and skills in a way that creates boundaries for success and practical solutions. The goal of this playbook is, over the next 30 days, for you to allocate 15 minutes each day to think, journal, and discuss the featured topic. You may not do it in 30 straight days. No big deal. You may want to iron out something with someone else before you move on. Great. When we prepare for a game, we build a plan. We must have the game plan in place before the starting whistle blows.

The following 30 plays are based around the acronym E.X.P.A.N.D. Each letter in E.X.P.A.N.D. represents an aspect of our lives – E is for experience, X is for the x-factor (heart), P is for personality and people skills, A is for authority, N is for Nurture and D is for direction. You will spend five days focusing on each of the six major themes. By participating in and reflecting on each day's activities, you will begin down the road to a more fulfilling life! All that's required of you is to set aside 7.5 hours of total preparation (30 reading days x 15 minutes). I don't think that's a bad investment, and hopefully you'll agree. After all, you're preparing for the most important game you'll ever play -- the game of your life.

E = Experience:

The building blocks of any organization, corporation, academic institution, or person are the experiences they have through their encounters with the world. Experience comes in many shapes and sizes. There are spiritual, educational, work, and relational experiences just to name a few. Experiences can be fun, sad, positive, negative, uplifting or painful.

For the next five days, let's try to make sense of our experiences and create awareness about how we make experience-based decisions. We live in a world of uncertainty, but that doesn't mean we can't have clarity. We can attain clarity of vision and action through experience. And thankfully, as well as learning on our own, we can also use the experiences of others as mileposts and moments of insight along the way.

Day One: Living in the Here and Now

<u>Quote</u>: "Obsession with the past and the fear of the future is the thief of today." -- Mark Twain

We need to answer one fundamental question in our lives. Why am I here? To find that answer, to discover our purpose for living, to develop clarity of vision, to reach goals, to challenge ourselves, and to live with a passion that drives us to fulfillment, we have to spend each day in the here and now. This doesn't mean that we are not affected by the past or not interested in the future. It means that the here and now is where it all starts. We can't measure the race and the finish line without a starting block. We need a place to push off from and get going. We need a launching pad, and then we can blast-off!

Key Thought for the Day: <u>Are you living in the NOW?</u>

Scripture of the Day: <u>This is the day which the LORD hath made; we will rejoice and be glad in it. (Psalm 118:24)</u>

Please write your responses to the following questions.

What is the past memory—either a single event or a period of time—that most often comes into your mind?

_____
_____
_____
_____
_____
_____

Is this a positive or a negative memory? Explain

_____
_____
_____
_____
_____
_____

Generally speaking, is your past something you long to relive or a time that fills you with unpleasant feelings? Explain.

_____
_____
_____
_____
_____
_____

Do you consciously choose to think about the past rather than the present or the future? Why? Why not?

_____
_____
_____
_____
_____
_____

If there anything or anyone in your past that makes you feel as if life will never be that good again? If so, briefly explain.

_____
_____
_____
_____
_____
_____
_____

How can living in the past become counterproductive to living a fulfilled life?

_____
_____
_____
_____
_____
_____
_____

What might you do to move beyond the past and focus on the present?

_____
_____
_____
_____
_____
_____
_____

Are there any future plans, events or "if only" dreams that are distracting you from being fully engaged in the present? If so, what?

_____
_____
_____
_____
_____
_____
_____

Are your thoughts about the future usually hopeful or fearful?

_____
_____
_____
_____
_____
_____
_____

What is wrong with "If Only" thinking?

_____
_____
_____
_____
_____
_____
_____

Do you feel that your future is going to be better than the past or present? Explain

_____
_____

_____
_____
_____
_____
_____

Does envisioning, fearing or otherwise obsessing about the future distract you or hinder you? If so in what way?

_____
_____
_____
_____
_____
_____

Journal your thoughts about today's Scripture: *This is the day the LORD has made; we will rejoice and be glad in it. (Ps 8:24)*

_____
_____
_____
_____
_____
_____

Living in the present can't be accomplished by just spending some time each day in self-reflection. Living in the present is coming to the understanding that we must also help others who need to be touched by the awesome power and mercy of the Creator. We are like a cup, and God wants to pour himself into us until our cup runs over with his spirit. We are called to keep our cup clean because only then can God change us with his abundant grace, and only then can we be fit to impact others and create a life of purpose for ourselves.

Dear Lord, help me enjoy the gifts of today. Show me how to remain thankful for the past but to stay in the present. Help me to love others today as you in your abundant mercy have loved me.

Day Two: Experience All Aspects of Life

"The glory of God is man fully alive." – St. Irenaeus of Lyon

Experiences come in many shapes and sizes but fall into five major categories: painful, educational, work, spiritual, and ministry experiences. Today we want to use our playbook to reflect upon the experiences that make up our lives because it is from experience that we gather insight for our game plan.

Painful experiences: "Pain is inevitable, misery is an option" a wise man once stated. It doesn't feel good to think about pain. But pain, when properly addressed, can lead to remarkable lives of accomplishment. We can find fulfillment by using our past pain to help others dealing pain of their own. For example, a woman who was raped can counsel unwed pregnant teens. A man who lost almost everything to alcohol abuse can change lives by running support groups. It is not only our pain, but our response to the pain that holds the key.

Educational experiences: Education is a catalyst. In order to grow as a person you must learn. We can get this process moving with education. It allows us to get out of neutral and into first gear. It also helps us take away our fear of failure. As they say knowledge is power. We can empower ourselves by using what we learn. This knowledge will increase our confidence as we journey through life.

Work experiences: There is a difference between success at work and significance at work. Winston Churchill said, "I make a living by what I get and a life by what I give." Work is a leverage tool. It increases our capacity to help others. This is a big deal! How can we work in such a way as to create a legacy for ourselves that lasts much longer than our chronological lives ever will?

Spiritual experiences: How we relate to and acknowledge our Creator has huge ramifications. If you don't share the belief that you were designed by the Creator of all things, exploring your own uniqueness becomes more difficult. Realizing that we were made "in His image and likeness" helps us not only to understand ourselves, but to know Him and begin to grasp His purpose for us—a unique purpose based on the distinctive way He designed each of us.

Ministry experiences: These are the works that we do for no other reason but to help others and glorify God. We just show up and serve. We act for the good of others without any thought of reward. We exercise kindness, mercy, and hospitality at the expense of self. In doing so, we join others who are changing the world for the better.

Key Thought for the Day: <u>We owe it to ourselves to fully experience the many aspects of our lives</u>

Scripture of the Day: <u>And we know that in all things God works for the good of those who love him, who have been called according to his purpose. (Romans 8:28)</u>

We will start with what most of us think of as life's biggest challenge: the things that hurt. Please write your responses to the following questions.

What are the three most painful experiences that you have gone through in the past?

1._____
_____

2._____
_____

3._____
_____

Are you going through a painful experience right now? If yes, please explain:

_____
_____
_____
_____
_____
_____
_____

How have you coped with these difficult experiences? Have you willingly faced them? Or have you somehow managed to avoid or evade them? Please explain.

_____
_____
_____
_____
_____
_____
_____

What are some coping skills that you might use to face these painful experiences?

_____
_____
_____
_____
_____
_____
_____

How can we use what we've learned from our painful experiences to help others?

_____
_____
_____
_____
_____
_____
_____
_____

Now let's think about your education or other learning experiences. Are you being "educated" by some of your present circumstances? Why or Why not?

_____
_____
_____
_____
_____
_____
_____
_____

Do you think you are making the most of your education and your learning experiences? Or do you think perhaps you are deflecting, avoiding or otherwise not experiencing them fully?

_____
_____
_____
_____
_____
_____
_____
_____

How can you use your education and other learning experiences to benefit others?

_____
_____
_____
_____
_____
_____
_____

What are the three most significant work experiences have you had in the past (if you a wife and mother that works at home, please don't assume that you don't "work!")?

1._____
_____

2._____
_____

3._____
_____

Why were these experiences significant?

_____
_____
_____
_____
_____
_____
_____

Do you think you have made the most of these experiences? Why? Why not?

_____
_____
_____
_____
_____
_____
_____

Is the part of you life that involves work is a good experience? Or a not-so-pleasant one? Why? And what might you do to make your work more rewarding?

_____
_____
_____
_____
_____
_____
_____

Let's take a moment now to think about our spiritual lives. What is the most significant spiritual experience you've ever had? Or, what is the most important spiritual lesson you have ever learned?

_____
_____
_____
_____
_____
_____
_____

What was the effect of this experience on your life? Did it make a difference in your behavior or your philosophy? Please explain

_____
_____
_____
_____
_____
_____
_____

How can you best use what you've learned to serve God?

_____
_____
_____
_____
_____
_____
_____

What does the word "ministry" mean to you? Have you ever been involved in it? If so, in what way?

_____
_____
_____
_____
_____
_____
_____

Was this a good experience? Why? Why not?

_____
_____

_____
_____
_____
_____
_____
_____

What If you could be involved in any ministry in the world, what would you most like to do?

_____
_____
_____
_____
_____
_____
_____
_____

Journal your thoughts about today's Scripture: *And we know that in all things God works for the good of those who love him, who have been called according to his purpose (Romans 8:28)*

_____
_____
_____
_____
_____
_____
_____
_____
_____
_____
_____
_____
_____

_____

_____

_____

_____

_____

_____

By fulfilling all five aspects of experience we orient our game plan in the direction of others. We shift our focus from self to the service of the many. The present will come alive for us as we impact others for the sake of good

Thank you for all my experiences whether painful, educational, work-related, spiritual, or ministry oriented. Thanks for your healing grace and for making me unique in your eyes. Allow these experiences to shape how I serve and help those who need me. I pray that I will show your love through my actions. Help me to respond in love by your grace.

Day Three: What have your experiences taught you?

Quote: "You are the sum total of all your decisions and experiences." -- Doug Bailey

Welcome back! I hope, as the days go by, that this playbook will become more and more alive for you. I'm glad you have made it to day three. You are already creating a new experience by disciplining yourself to be still and draw near to God.

Past experiences help us set boundaries. One lesson that I hope you will take away from your playbook today is that we can all learn not only from our own past experiences, but also from the past experiences of others. That's why learning to listen is so important. For example, if you're married with two kids under age 5, why not find a mentor who has been married 20 years longer with kids over 25? The experiences of others can be very helpful to you. By building your own personal "board of directors" comprised of wise and experienced friends, you can shorten your own learning curve.

Besides listening, we also need to take time to stop and think. If you want your current experience to be optimal, the absolute best, why not reflect before taking action? Spend some quiet time going through the following questions. Remember, game plans and playbooks adjust with circumstances and events. Take the time to create a plan that will lead to a desired outcome.

When we take action it leads to experience, and each experience impacts all aspects of our lives, including the ultimate outcome. Why not make each experience special for you and others? You can do this by conditioning your mind and your heart. Let's get started.

Key Thought for the Day: <u>We must learn from our experiences.</u>

Scripture of the Day: <u>Because of the LORD's great love…his compassions never fail. They are new every morning; great is your faithfulness. (Lamentations 3:22-23)</u>

Please write your responses to the following questions.

First let's take a moment and look at the past. What are the three most significant experiences you've ever had?

1._____
_____

2._____
_____

3._____
_____

Explain why you chose each of these specific experiences

1._____
_____

2._____
_____

3._____
_____

What did you learn from these experiences?
_____
_____
_____
_____
_____

If you are really honest with yourself, do you believe that you have taken what you learned from these things and used it to improve your life? Why? Why not?

Did you sense God's presence while you were going through these experiences?
Explain.

Describe some ways you might be able to use what you've learned from your experiences to serve God and others?

_____
_____

Now let's take a look at the present. What are the most significant experiences you are going through right now (there may be more or less than three)?

1._____
_____

2._____
_____

3._____
_____

Have you sensed God's presence in the midst of these important experiences? Please explain

_____
_____
_____
_____
_____
_____
_____

Describe an experience in your life where you have recognized the compassion or faithfulness of God

_____
_____
_____
_____
_____
_____

_____
_____
_____
_____
_____
_____
_____

Journal your thoughts about today's Scripture: *Because of the LORD's great love…his compassions never fail. They are new every morning; great is your faithfulness.*

_____
_____
_____
_____
_____
_____
_____
_____
_____
_____
_____
_____
_____
_____

Experiences are the building blocks of our lives. They come from daily encounters with other people as well as from influences such as novels, plays, songs, scripture, history, reflection and memory. What will you do today to make sure your experiences can be used to impact others for the good?

Thank you Lord for a day full of experiences, for without them life would be empty and incomplete. I pray that the greatest experience of today is to be with you, to draw into the sanctuary of your love today and always.

Day Four: What new experiences do you fear?

Quote: Fear that is submerged, disguised, or otherwise bottled up inside us acts as a secret damper on whole areas of the mind. But fear honestly felt and openly expressed is a sign of mental health and may even aid in discovery. – Robert Grudin

Did you know that you're only born with two natural fears? Yes, just two! Any guesses? The only fears that a baby has are the fear of falling and the fear of loud noises. All other fears are learned. Let that sink in. ALL fears that you have, ALL burdens that you carry are learned.

Today let's think about how we can rely on God to handle our fears.

Key Thought for the Day: You must be able to openly face your fears.

Scripture of the Day: Therefore do not worry about tomorrow, for tomorrow will worry about itself. Each day has enough trouble of its own. (Matthew 6:34)

Please write your responses to the following questions.

Stop and think for a moment about things in the future that frighten you the most. What are they?

_____
_____
_____
_____
_____
_____
_____

Have you ever felt so afraid of something that you thought you couldn't face it? If so, when, and what was the outcome?

_____
_____
_____
_____
_____
_____
_____

Why do you think fear can become such a crippling emotion?

_____
_____
_____
_____
_____
_____
_____

What have you done in the past to help confront and overcome your fears of the future?

_____
_____
_____
_____
_____
_____
_____

How can we turn our fears into positive experiences?

_____
_____

Why do your think it is important to experience new things?

How can you most effectively confront your fears?

Once you have confronted your fear and overcome it, how can you most effectively apply the experience to improve the rest of your life?

_____

_____

Journal your thoughts about today's Scripture: *Therefore do not worry about tomorrow, for tomorrow will worry about itself. Each day has enough trouble of its own. (Matthew 6:34)*

_____

_____

_____

_____

_____

_____

_____

_____

_____

_____

_____

_____

_____

Military service personnel have a tried and true saying, "You fight like you train." Do you believe some fears, not all, can be overcome by training? Sure. We see it in sports all the time. The gymnast can't do the back flip on the beam in competition until she first practices it on the low beam in a harness. Then she moves on to a higher beam and harness. Then finally onto the regulation height with the harness removed. We see only the finished skill, not the dedication and determination to overcome the fear of a blind landing. It is by faithful practice to the proper skills that the movement of a back flip on a beam is even attempted, much less nailed cold in competition. What fears can you train away with God's help? Training helps, but having a training partner to hold us accountable to overcoming our fears is mandatory.

Lord, you have said, "Fear not for I am with you." Help me to draw near to you so I can live free of fear. Let me love you, Lord, more everyday.

Day Five: What new experiences do you most desire?

Quote: There was a disturbance in my heart, a voice that spoke there and said, I want, I want, I want! It happened every afternoon, and when I tried to suppress it it got even stronger. It never said a thing except I want, I want, I want! – Saul Bellow from Henderson the Rain King.

Saul Bellow's quote cuts to the heart of human craving. We see a similar hunger in Psalm 73 where Asaph tells us that he is struggling with envy and jealousy as he looks upon the rich who, unlike him, seem to have everything. Life is good for them; they are healthy and content. He is getting physically sick because of his own situation when he turns to God and asks for His help. In response, God makes an extraordinary promise of change and fulfilled desire.

We live in a world where change is not only constant but inevitable. There isn't one cell in your body that was there seven years ago. They have all been replaced. Think about it. Not one cell. With God's help we can also renew ourselves in heart and spirit, and discover experiences unlike any we've had before. Try it today.

Key Thought for the Day: Use your desires to discover positive new experiences.

Scripture of the Day: Delight yourself in the LORD and he will give you the desires of your heart. (Psalm 37:4)

Please write your responses to the following questions.

In what ways can desire be a positive emotion?

_____

_____

In what ways can desire be a negative emotion?

Have your desires ever had a negative effect on your life? If so, explain.

How have your desires turned out to be blessings in your life?

What do you most wish for in the future?
_____
_____
_____
_____
_____
_____

Why is this desire so important to you?
_____
_____
_____
_____
_____
_____

Do you ever pray and ask God to give you the things you desire?
_____

Have you ever had a prayer answered? Describe what happened
_____
_____
_____
_____
_____
_____

Praying for God to grant us our desires almost always involves waiting and hoping and keeping faith. How can you most effectively allow the unfulfilled desires in your heart to have a positive impact on your life and on the lives of others?

___

How can you most effectively allow your desires to bring glory to God?

___

Journal your thoughts about today's Scripture: *Delight yourself in the LORD and he will give you the desires of your heart (Psalm 37:4)*

___

_____

_____

_____

New experiences – will you have any today? Will they be the result of your willingness to bring your heart's desire to God, humbling yourself and asking for His help? As your circumstances begin to change, use your experience for the good of others. It makes life so much more rewarding and fun. Remember like a new play, a new experience can add variety to your playbook as well as turning you into a winner.

Father, help me to process new experiences without wanting what everyone else has that I don't. Help me to know you and make every day a new and renewing experience with you.

The X-factor: Heart

When I first got married, first held my son and my daughter in my arms, and first lost a close loved one, my heart was affected. In times of deep emotion, we discover that the heart not just a muscle that pumps blood, but is a name for the part of us that contains our passions, dreams, and desires. We can have all the vision we want, but without the passion to execute it we cannot and will not overcome the natural obstacles of life.

We've heard the phrases, "the heart of an athlete," "heart of a giver," or "heart of one who would change the world for the better." Our heart drives our behavior. It creates energy. Heart gets people excited. When we say, "She's all heart," we mean that her ability alone is not enough. Heart drives what we say, how we feel, and how we act. How can we explore our heart?

Let's take the next five days to explore the "x-factor" in your life.

Day Six: What is heart? Heart is character.

Quote: "Be the change you wish to see in the world." – Mahatma Gandhi

At the heart of the x-factor is genuine concern for others. We must have positive, healthy feelings for those around us. As mentioned on day one, when we are right with God our cup runs over with his grace and love and positively affects the relationships and people we are closest to! Most people are desperate for encouragement, unconditional love, and reaffirmation. Let's explore how our hearts can be directed to help those who are empty.

Key Thought for the Day: Purify your heart and strengthen your character with God's help.

Scripture of the Day: Create in me a pure heart, O God, and renew a steadfast spirit within me. (Psalm 51:10)

Please write your responses to the following questions.

When we say someone has "a good heart" we usually mean that he or she has a good character. Describe what having a "good character" means and why it is important.

_____
_____
_____
_____
_____
_____

What are your five most positive character traits?
1._____
_____
2._____
_____
3._____
_____
4._____
_____
5._____
_____

Give an example of how one of these qualities has benefited your life or the life of someone else.

_____
_____
_____
_____
_____
_____
_____

What are your top five negative character traits?
1._____
_____
2._____
_____
3._____
_____
4._____
_____

5._____
_____

How might you minimize the influence of the five negatives characteristics on your thoughts and behavior?

1._____
_____

2._____
_____

3._____
_____

4._____
_____

5._____
_____

How can you most effectively use your five best character traits to have a positive impact on the lives of others?

1._____
_____

2._____
_____

3._____
_____

4._____
_____

5._____
_____

How can recognizing the strengths and weaknesses in your character draw you closer to God?

___

Journal your thoughts about today's Scripture: *Create in me a pure heart, O God, and renew a steadfast spirit within me. Psalm 51:10*

___

Do you ever picture yourself as someone else? Maybe Abraham Lincoln, Martin Luther King Jr., or Mother Teresa. Or maybe a great athlete, teacher, or even your own doctor. Your heart can make you—like some of these people who have made our world a better place—a pioneer to a new way of living. Heart makes it possible for us to give a helping hand to others. What's in our heart shapes our character.

Open the eyes to my heart Lord
Open the eyes to my heart.
I want to see you
I want to see you...

Day Seven: To develop your character, get in touch with your emotions.

Quote: To lie to oneself about one's potential development…is one of the most insidious daily inner gnawings a person can experience, and a great source of baffling, generalized guilt. – Ernst Becker, *The Denial of Death*

Wow, "Getting in touch with who we are." I never liked that phrase much. Nevertheless, it is an important concept. Perhaps we can make the idea more appealing by putting it in different words. How about, "Taking the time to discover how God made me"? This is something we all must do. Yet, it can seem nearly impossible sometimes. We spend our waking hours doing so many things: working, going to movies, hanging out with friends, falling in love. You might say that we spend life as a category 5 tornado going from one thing to the next. And sometimes it's nearly impossible to slow that tornado down!

But we must be mature enough to search ourselves daily. We must explore our thoughts and feelings—not because we need to be in a performance-based place everyday, but because we need to be in a relationship-based place. We need to be free from guilt, shame, and burnout. We need to try to eliminate all those negative emotions because they hold us back from having a healthy relationship with God and with others. Enjoy this section, be still, and let God work.

Key Thought for the Day: Get in touch with your emotions.

Scripture of the Day: Search me, O God and know my heart; test me and know my anxious thoughts. (Psalm 139:23)

Please write your responses to the following questions.

What do emotions have to do with character?

_____
_____
_____
_____
_____
_____
_____

What does it mean to be "in touch" with your emotions?

_____
_____
_____
_____
_____
_____
_____

Do you believe that you are in touch with your emotions? Why? Why not?

_____
_____
_____
_____
_____
_____

What negative emotion(s) do you find yourself experiencing most often?

_____
_____
_____
_____
_____
_____
_____

How do you typically react when you experience these emotions?

_____
_____
_____
_____
_____
_____
_____

Do you believe that this is the best response to the emotion(s)? Why? Why not?

_____
_____
_____
_____
_____
_____
_____

How can turning to God for help enable us to deal with our emotions and the negative behaviors they sometimes lead to?

_____
_____
_____
_____
_____
_____
_____

What positive emotion(s) do you find yourself experiencing most often?

_____
_____
_____
_____
_____
_____
_____

How do you typically react when you experience these emotions?

_____
_____
_____
_____
_____
_____
_____

Do you believe that this is the proper response to the emotion(s)? Why? Why not?

_____
_____
_____
_____
_____
_____
_____

How can increased awareness of our emotions better develop our character?

_____
_____
_____
_____
_____
_____
_____

Journal your thoughts about today's Scripture: *Search me, O God, and know my heart; test me and know my anxious thoughts. (Psalm 139:23)*.

_____
_____
_____
_____
_____
_____
_____
_____
_____

_____

_____

_____

_____

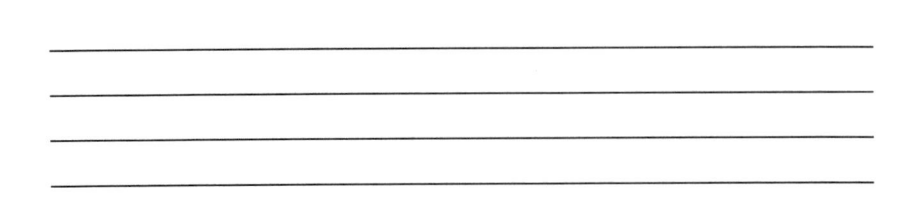

What have you learned about yourself so far? There were probably a lot of questions—maybe more questions than answers. And you can be sure that all the answers won't necessarily be available to you right away, because this matter of getting in touch with our emotions is a life-long process, not an event. So take the first step, open yourself up and be the Christopher Columbus of your own life. Set sail, explore, discover, and in the process I believe you'll begin to find out why you're here.

Lord, help me to have peace in my soul and let me be still as I sit with you. Wipe out my transgressions and set me free to feel my true emotions, so that I can more authentically serve you and love others.

Day Eight: Reflect, Don't React

Quote: "Set goals outside of your current work. Begin to pursue these goals now." -- Peter Drucker

The alarm rings, we grab a pop-tart and we are out the door in just three-and-a-half minutes flat! Must be a little over-scheduled, huh? How do we slow down enough to reflect on our actions instead of rushing or reacting? It's a discipline to find the time daily to plan and create a vision for our lives. Great generals plan, great coaches plan, great teachers, leaders, moms and dads plan. We must learn how to calm down, take a deep breath, and start reflecting instead of reacting. Let's take a look at some questions that may help.

Key Thought for the Day: Personal growth, health, and well-being comes through reflection.

Scripture of the Day: Everyone should be quick to listen, slow to speak and slow to become angry. (James 1:19)

Please write your responses to the following questions.

Do you think of yourself as unemotional, somewhat emotional or very emotional?

_____

Has anyone ever told you that you are over-reactive or said that you have a "short fuse?"

_____

How do you tend to react when faced with good news, a compliment or other positive experiences?

_____
_____
_____
_____
_____
_____
_____

How do you typically react to insults, criticism or personal slights?

_____
_____
_____
_____
_____
_____
_____

What are some ways your reactions might have (or have had) an adverse effect on your life?

_____
_____
_____
_____
_____
_____
_____

Would you consider yourself a reflective person? Why? Why not?

_____
_____

_____
_____
_____
_____
_____

Do you think having a reflective nature is a good thing? If so, how can a person become more reflective?

_____
_____
_____
_____
_____
_____
_____

What are the benefits of reflection vs. reaction?

_____
_____
_____
_____
_____
_____
_____

List five things you could do to slow down your reaction time and become more reflective:

1._____
_____

2._____
_____

3._____
_____
4._____
_____
5._____
_____

How can our personal faith in God make a difference in the way we respond to both the good and bad things that come into our lives?

_____
_____
_____
_____
_____
_____

Journal your thoughts about today's Scripture: *Everyone should be quick to listen, slow to speak and slow to become angry.* (*James 1:19*)

_____
_____
_____
_____
_____
_____
_____
_____
_____
_____

_____

_____

Reflection is essential to living a life of significance. Reaction just leads to chaos. Unplanned reaction will never benefit you in the way that planned reflection will. The person who reflects is able to move ahead. The one who simply reacts remains stuck in same place, tires spinning in the emotional mud, never moving.

Please hear me, Lord, as I ask you to help me make my days quiet and still so I can reflect and allow you to guide me. Let me trust you more and more to give me the vision I need. Help me meet you daily.

Day Nine: Choose peace over possessions.

Quote: "I've got all the money I ever need for a house, but it won't buy me a home. I've got all the money I ever need for a companion, but it won't buy me love. And I've got all the money I ever need for a bed, but it won't buy me a good night's sleep." – Zig Ziglar

Welcome to getting rid of what you think you want or need and, instead, finding peace of mind. Today let's focus on the difference between what I get and what I give. Which one lasts longer when applied to the relationships in your life that really matter? How can we have peace in an insanely possession-based society? Only a peaceful person will make time to help others, care for the weak, and love the lonely.

Peace of mind or peace of self comes from living a transparent life—a life where we are conscious of our thoughts and emotions, honest with ourselves and others, unhindered by hidden agendas, and truthful and straightforward with God. Let's try these questions on for size.

Key Thought for the Day: Choose peace over possessions.

Scripture of the Day: You will keep him in perfect peace, whose mind is stayed on You, because he trusts in You. (Isaiah 26:3)

Of all your personal possessions, which ones do you love the most and why?

_____
_____
_____
_____
_____
_____

In what ways are material possessions good things?

_____
_____
_____
_____
_____
_____

In what ways are they not so good?

_____
_____
_____
_____
_____
_____

What are some ways that your efforts to increase your personal possessions have had an adverse effect on you?

_____
_____
_____
_____
_____
_____

Would you say that you have peace of mind? Why? Why not?

_____
_____
_____

Can our desire for personal possessions and our efforts to gain them have an adverse effect on our spiritual lives? Explain

What are the primary benefits of inner peace?

Can you think of some ways you might gain more peace of mind?

What steps could you take to become less focused on possessions and more able to experience inner peace?

_____
_____
_____
_____
_____
_____
_____

Journal your thoughts about today's Scripture: *You will keep him in perfect peace, whose mind is stayed on You, because he trusts in You. (Isaiah 26:3)*

_____
_____
_____
_____
_____
_____
_____
_____
_____
_____
_____
_____
_____
_____

You see, possessions can be wonderful, but peace comes from setting our hearts apart from all the things that hold us, letting go of our material attachments, and living in the love and service of others. As we consider the conflict that brews between relationships and things, it all becomes so clear. Healthy relationships calm us, and bring peace to our lives.

Oh merciful God. Forgive me of my lust for things. Please help me find my way to peace. Help me stop looking at what I can get and strengthen my belief in helping others today. Let your love overflow to touch all those who I meet today.

Day Ten: Become more Christ-like in your heart.

Quote: "Really believe in your heart of hearts that your fundamental purpose, the reason for being is to enlarge the lives of others. Your life will be enlarged also. And all of the other things we have been taught to concentrate on will take care of themselves." -- Pete Thigpen, *Executive Reserves*

Studies show that 68% of all relationships, whether personal or business, end because one or both parties feels ignored. By becoming more like Christ and studying his way and interactions with the people of his day, we see a man who knew how to stay connected. Jesus understood his calling. He trusted God and was patient. He surrendered his ambitions for God's purpose. Because he did those things by design, he never had to worry about those who were lost -- he was drawn to them.

Key Thought for the Day: Choose to become more like Christ.

Scripture of the Day: <u>If anyone obeys his word, God's love is truly made complete in him. This is how we know we are in him: Whoever claims to live in him must walk as Jesus did. (I John 2:5-6)</u>

Please write your responses to the following questions:

Why do you think God wants us to become more Christ-like?

_____
_____
_____
_____
_____

_____

_____

How can being more like Christ benefit us in our daily lives?

_____
_____
_____
_____
_____
_____

Do you believe that you are making a good effort to become more like Christ? Why? Why not?

_____
_____
_____
_____
_____
_____

What would you consider to be three Christ-like qualities that are desirable to you? After listing them, write a brief explanation of why they are appealing to you.

1._____

_____

2._____

_____

3._____

_____

What are the three Christ-like qualities you most identify with and that you believe may be part of your character?

1._____

_____

2._____

_____

3._____

_____

Now let's focus on improvement. What are three qualities of Christ that you believe are most lacking your character?

1._____

_____

2._____

_____

3._____

_____

What steps might you take to successfully foster within yourself each of these Christ-like qualities?

1._____

_____

_____

2._____

_____

_____

3._____

_____

_____

Journal your thoughts about today's Scripture: *If anyone obeys his word, God's love is truly made complete in him. This is how we know we are in him: Whoever claims to live in him must walk as Jesus did. (I John 2:5-6)*

_____
_____
_____
_____
_____
_____
_____
_____
_____
_____
_____
_____
_____

In order to become more Christ-like we must develop our character from within. With dedication and perseverance, we can begin to create the positive character traits that Christ wants us to have. We also need to remember that prayer has the power to change our hearts and to let that change positively affect our relationships and daily lives.

Lord God, soften my heart. Burn away the hardness of my soul. Help me to have a Christ-like heart and let today be the day I feel and know that my life can be changed by your love. Allow me the honor of taking and sharing that change with others. In your almighty name I pray, Amen.

P= Personality and People Skills

A very great leader of men, General George C. Marshall, chief of the U.S. Army during World War II, had a remarkable record of putting people in the right place at the right time. He developed and promoted over 600 people to ranks of divisional commander. He did it by focusing on the strengths not the weaknesses of each person.

With that in mind, we are going to will focus on personality and people skills for the next five days. Just as General Marshall took leaders and trained them in roles that accentuated their strengths, let's set some objectives for this section that allow us to optimize strength, turn weakness into power, and strengthen our relationships with others—all through training.

Day Eleven: Develop Your Abilities by Identifying Your Personality's Strengths

Quote: We lead by being human. We do not lead by being corporate, professional, or institutional." -- Paul G Hawken, founder of *Smith and Hawken*

As you delve into today's questions, remember that these should be different from the answers you gave on day ten. Look at today as being personality-oriented rather than character-oriented. For example, you should explore whether you are outgoing or introverted. Perhaps you are more competitive than cooperative. Think about and answer the questions based on that type of thinking. You may want to talk with someone you trust and ask them if they think your answers are on track.

Key Thought for the Day: Take a few moments to identify the strengths of your personality.

Scripture of the Day: <u>For you created my inmost being; you knit me together in my mother's womb. I praise you because I am fearfully and wonderfully made; your works are wonderful. (Psalm 139:13-14)</u>

Please write your responses to the following questions:

What are your three best personality traits?
1._____
_____
_____
2._____
_____
_____

3._____
_____
_____

For each trait, describe a situation in which having this personality trait benefited the outcome of your actions.

1._____
_____
_____

2._____
_____
_____

3._____
_____
_____

Now think about the times in which you might have been able to use your personality strengths to your advantage, but for whatever reason you did not. List three of them here:

1._____
_____
_____

2._____
_____
_____

3._____
_____
_____

For each situation, describe why you think you didn't use your personality strengths to your advantage; this could have been a conscious choice, or perhaps you weren't able to do it even if you had wanted to.

1. _____
_____
_____

2. _____
_____
_____

3. _____
_____
_____

In what ways can you further develop your personality strengths?
_____
_____
_____
_____
_____
_____

How might you go about ensuring that in the future you always use your personality strengths to benefit your life?
_____
_____
_____
_____
_____
_____

Journal your thoughts about today's Scripture: *For you created my inmost being; you knit me together in my mother's womb. I praise you because I am fearfully and wonderfully made; your works are wonderful. (Psalm 139:13-14)*

_____
_____
_____
_____
_____
_____
_____
_____
_____
_____
_____
_____
_____
_____

Personality strengths can drive us to new highs, but their flip-side, personality weaknesses, can send us plummeting to new lows. With God's grace we can learn to use our strengths, to avoid negative relationships and situations and to live effective and purposeful lives.

God, help me understand how I was made so I can discover your will for my personality. Allow me to find discernment and understanding into how you made me. Help me in the struggles that come my way because of who I am. Let me know you more clearly everyday so that I can better know myself.

Day Twelve: Identify Your Personality's Weaknesses and Change Them into Strengths

Quote: *I never see hurdles. Only the finish line. – Edwin Moses, Olympic Champion*

Today is an opportunity to think about some of your weaknesses. Things like anger, envy, jealousy, lack of self-discipline, lack of focus, whatever they may be. Can you imagine being able to change these weaknesses into strengths? Let's take a closer look at that idea. Whatever we do, we'll finish out the day by leaving our weaknesses at the cross. There is no reason to keep carrying them around as if they're a burden that we can't get rid of.

Keep in mind that you'll probably never be able to overcome *all* of your weaknesses. It's just not realistic. Instead, take the words of Edwin Moses to heart and focus on the finish line. By zeroing-in on where you want to be at the end, you'll be more willing and able to achieve your goal: turning weakness into strength.

Key Thought for the Day: Take time to identify the weaknesses of your personality.

Scripture of the Day: That is why, for Christ's sake, I delight in weaknesses, in insults, in hardships, in persecutions, in difficulties. For when I am weak, then I am strong. (I Corinthians 12:10)

Please write your responses to the following questions:

What are, in your opinion, your three most obvious negative personality traits?

1._____
_____
_____

2._____
_____
_____

3._____
_____
_____

For each trait, describe a situation in which having this personality trait has negatively influenced the outcome of your actions.

1._____
_____
_____

2._____
_____
_____

3._____
_____
_____

Now think about a time in which you have been able to overcome one of these personality weaknesses to benefit your life

_____
_____
_____
_____

_____

_____

_____

What steps could you take to change your three personality weaknesses into strengths?

1._____

_____

_____

2._____

_____

_____

3._____

_____

_____

Why is it important to both understand and confront your personality's weaknesses?

_____

_____

_____

_____

_____

_____

How can your faith in God help you transform your personality weaknesses into strengths?

_____

_____

_____

Journal your thoughts about today's Scripture: *That is why, for Christ's sake, I delight in weaknesses, in insults, in hardships, in persecutions, in difficulties. For when I am weak, then I am strong. (I Corinthians 12:10)*

Needless to say, we all have weaknesses. There are some weaknesses that we, quite frankly, may never entirely get over, through, or around. They may gnaw and nag at us for years. We should adopt the mindset that given enough time, attention and effort, it is possible to turn them into strengths. How about today, right now, letting your worst weaknesses go? Turn them over to God. We're not in this alone!

If there was ever a time, Lord, that you could just catch me and hold me in your arms it's now. There are things that I've messed up, weaknesses that burden me, fears that control me. It is in this humbled state that I come to you Lord God. Please, transform my weakness into strength and let it burden me no more.

Day Thirteen: Focus on what People Matter the Most to You and Why.

Quote: "Success, like happiness, cannot be pursued; it must ensue, and it only does so as an unintended side effect of one's personal dedication to a cause greater than oneself or as the by-product of one's surrender to a person other than oneself." – Victor Frankl

As I age, the discovery that has been the most exciting to me is that I don't have to be loved by everyone I meet. This is a new awareness—there was a time when being loved and accepted mattered very much. Now I only want to be loved by a chosen few—those that God has put in my life as a gift.

My cup overflows with love, affection, and kindness for these chosen few people that mean everything to me. George McGovern, a former presidential candidate, lost a daughter who froze to death in a snow bank. At the zenith of his political career he said that he would willingly give it all away for one more moment with her; a lunch, a laugh, or a hug. Take a moment to reflect on your nearest and dearest loved ones.

Key Thought for the Day: Discover what people matter the most to you and why.

Scripture of the Day: No one has ever seen God; but if we love one another, God lives in us and his love is made complete in us. (I John 4:11-13)

Please write your responses to the following questions.

Let's start today by naming the five most important people in your life:

1._____

2._____

3._____

4._____

5._____

Now let's take the time to fully describe why each person is so special to you.

1._____

2._____

3._____

4._____

5._____

Why is it so important to focus on other people rather than yourself?

What three aspects of yourself or your life do you ordinarily end up focusing your time and energy on (these might be things like appearance, success, dating, hobbies, etc.)

1._____

2._____

3._____

Why do you think you focus so much attention on these things?

What can you do to effectively shift your focus away from yourself and onto the people who matter the most to you?

Journal your thoughts about today's Scripture: *No one has ever seen God; but if we love one another, God lives in us and his love is made complete in us.* (I John 4:11-13)

By now I think you know who is really important in your life. First take a moment to thank God for them. Then go spend time with them. Go!

Give me the discernment, dear God, to know what relationships you want me in and let me pour myself into those that you bring to my attention. Help me to see everyone I meet through your eyes, from the perspective of eternity.

Day Fourteen: Choose People Over Pleasure.

Quote: "May the cup of God's grace overflow into the lives of people you touch." -- Mark Warren

Mother Teresa made a difference in the world by choosing people over pleasure. Helping the poor was her lifelong calling and she embraced it with passion and purpose. Today you can do the same thing. You're probably thinking, "Wait a minute, I'm no Mother Teresa." Well maybe not, but we can all learn from her example. Turn the TV or iPod off and have a 15 minute uninterrupted conversation with one of those five or so people you discovered on day 13. Think of some people you know who have chosen people over pleasure. Isn't it true that their life is consistently rich and full of joy? Enjoy today. Enjoy the people.

Key Thought for the Day: It is essential that we choose people over pleasure in order to have a fulfilling life.

Scripture of the Day: The King will reply, 'I tell you the truth, whatever you did for one of the least of these brothers of mine, you did for me.'" (Matthew 25:40)

Please write your responses to the following questions:

What are three experiences in which some particular pleasure, and/or your pursuit of it, has had a negative impact on your life?

1._____
_____
_____

2._____
_____
_____

3._____
_____
_____

Was anyone hurt by your actions? Explain
_____
_____
_____
_____
_____
_____
_____

Now describe how each of those negative experiences could have been made better if you had chosen people over pleasure.

1._____
_____
_____

2._____
_____
_____

3._____
_____
_____

Shifting gears: List three pleasures that you could either pursue or postpone today:

1._____
2._____
3._____

Is it essential for you to experience these pleasures today? Why? Why not?

_____
_____
_____
_____
_____
_____
_____

Instead of experiencing those three pleasures, choose three people who you would like to focus on caring for or helping out today:
1._____
2._____
3._____

In what ways could you reach out to each person?
Person #1

_____
_____
_____
_____
_____
_____
_____

Person #2

_____
_____
_____
_____

Person #3

Why is it important to God that we chose people over pleasure?

Journal your thoughts about today's Scripture: *The King will reply, 'I tell you the truth, whatever you did for one of the least of these brothers of mine, you did for me.'" (Matthew 25:40)*

_____

_____

_____

_____

_____

_____

_____

How did this section go? Can you find an action step that will allow you to be more like Mother Teresa than Madonna? When we give up pleasing ourselves for the sake of others, the Holy Spirit begins to move in our lives, guiding and directing us. Enjoy this rite of passage. Make a significant difference in who you are by investing in others.

Thank you God for you son, Jesus. He lived, learned, taught and ultimately gave up his life so we could be free of our addictions to pleasure. You are so awesome, God, to choose us over the pleasure of keeping your Son in heaven with you. Thanks for sharing the greatest gift of all with us.

Day Fifteen: Use things, not people.

<u>Quote:</u> "And in the end the love you take is equal to the love you make." – The Beatles

We need to see clearly the difference between using things and using people. We make things with our hands or buy things made by the hands of others. The underlying current here is we make *things*.

God is the only one who can make a *person*. We build a house, God builds us. We make a movie, God gives life real meaning. We have a job, God creates relationships that work. As you explore this concept, remember anything that we make can be used today, but anybody that God makes has eternal value, and is not intended for our exploitation. Focus today on identifying ways that you use people as if they were things, and then discovering how you can stop this behavior.

Key Thought for the Day: Use things, not people.

Scripture of the Day: <u>My command is this: Love each other as I have loved you. (John 15:12)</u>

Please write your responses to the following questions:

What does "using" another person mean to you?

_____
_____
_____
_____
_____
_____

What are some ways that you might convince yourself that using another person is an okay thing to do?

_____
_____
_____
_____
_____
_____
_____

Take a few minutes now to list three times when you took advantage of a person (or persons) in order to benefit yourself in some way:

1._____
_____
_____

2._____
_____
_____

3._____
_____
_____

For each event, describe why you used that person or persons. Were your actions planned? Were they done out of "necessity"? Try to put yourself in your own shoes at the time.

1._____
_____
_____

2._____
_____
_____

3._____
_____
_____

Now come up with three times that you felt used by another person or persons:

1._____
_____
_____

2._____
_____
_____

3._____
_____
_____

For each event, describe how you felt. What did you learn from that experience?

1._____
_____
_____

2._____
_____
_____

3._____
_____
_____

Why is it wrong to use other people to benefit ourselves? How is this behavior detrimental to our Christian lives?

_____
_____
_____
_____
_____
_____
_____

How might this behavior affect the example you set as a Christian?

_____
_____
_____
_____
_____
_____
_____

Journal your thoughts about today's Scripture: *My command is this: Love each other as I have loved you.* (John 15:12)

_____
_____
_____
_____
_____
_____
_____
_____
_____

_____

_____

_____

How did it feel when you answered the question "have you ever felt used?" God didn't intend that any of us should be treated like objects. We are, instead, living breathing men and women who should be treated with love, kindness, and respect. Those are desires common to all people; they are also desires inanimate objects don't possess. Things have no needs. People do. Do something today for someone who needs your special blessing.

Lord, help me to recognize the difference between your creation and my creation. Let me understand that your creation is to be respected and honored and that my creations should be simply enjoyed. Thank you, in advance, for the insight to know the difference.

A = Authority

What does it mean to submit to an authority? Does it mean we have to give up being who we are? What do we mean by the term "authority figure"? Is it a simply a powerful person to whom we must surrender our will? Is it a parent, boss, leader, pastor or priest? Authority is a universally understood concept; we have all been exposed to it in one form or another. Authority has to do with boundaries—boundaries that guide and shape our behavior in various situations. We need boundaries to do everything from operating a motor vehicle to loving the people who matter most to us.

When we are in a relationship with an honest and trustworthy authority figure, we have no need to worry about negative consequences. Even if we are under the authority of an unjust or unreasonable person or system, we are able live in peace of mind because God has promised to take care of the ultimate outcome. That's why there is no need for us to fear or rebel against authority. In fact, learning to submit to authority can lead us to great freedom. Over the next five chapters let's work on things like creating better relationships with authority, choosing to give authority to others, and seeking to recognize our ultimate authority.

Day Sixteen: Take a Day to Reflect on Authority.

<u>Quote:</u> "I always ask myself, 'Would I want one of my sons or daughters to work under that person?'" -- Peter Drucker

The first step in surrendering to God is to recognize earthly authorities who are bigger and more powerful than we are. God has placed certain people in authority over us, and by letting go of control, we can see that their authority is a tool that can help us succeed. Remember that authority is all about boundaries. Authority provides the rules of the game. We need these rules in our playbook; we just need to know where the rules apply and how we should play out the life we have been given.

Key Thought for the Day: Discover what "authority" really means to you.

Scripture of the Day: <u>If you are pleased with me, teach me your ways so I may know you and continue to find favor with you. (Exodus 33:13)</u>

Please write your responses to the following questions:

When you hear the word "authority" what do you think and feel?

_____
_____
_____
_____
_____
_____

How do you personally deal with authority? Do you handle it well, or are you rebellious towards it? Explain:

_____
_____
_____
_____
_____
_____
_____

Do you relate better to human authority figures or to non-living sources of authority such as the law or the Bible? Why?

_____
_____
_____
_____
_____
_____
_____

Do you think it is important for all of us to respect authority? Why or why not?

_____
_____
_____
_____
_____
_____
_____

Now let's talk about your life. List three ways that you are now or will someday become an authority figure to others.

1._____
_____

2._____
_____

3._____
_____

Do you believe that you do or will handle your authority properly? Why? Why not?

_____
_____
_____
_____
_____
_____
_____

How can your own responses to authority help you be a better authority figure?

_____
_____
_____
_____
_____
_____
_____

Journal your thoughts about today's Scripture: *If you are pleased with me, teach me your ways so I may know you and continue to find favor with you.* (Exodus 33:13)

_____
_____
_____
_____
_____
_____
_____
_____
_____
_____
_____
_____
_____
_____
_____
_____

What was the biggest discovery you made as you contemplated authority? For most of us it come in realizing that authority is something to run toward, not away from. By now I hope you're beginning to see that authority can direct our path and shape our purpose in a positive way. If you learn how to embrace authority, you will have taken the first steps towards learning how to put your complete trust in someone else.

Oh Lord Almighty, the ultimate authority, please help me to be more open to your rules and guidelines. Help me not to fear or resent the authority figures in my life, but instead teach me to welcome their presence and to enjoy the rewards of submitting, through them, to your perfect will. Thank you that your rules keep me in a meaningful relationship with you.

Day Seventeen: Create a Better Relationship with Authorities You Are Required to Answer To.

Quote: "A wise man will hear and increase learning." -- Proverbs 1:5

A conundrum we all face at one time or another is whether to feel entitled to something, or to graciously accept what is given to us. A sense of entitlement leads to selfishness, envy, and jealousy. It encourages us to believe that we set the rules in life. However, if we have a heart full of thanksgiving, we feel comfortable submitting to authority by humbly offering ourselves and receiving with gratitude the gifts we have been given. Let's check out the questions in the playbook.

Key Thought for the Day: Create a Better Relationship with the Authorities in Your Life

Scripture of the Day: Everyone must submit himself to the governing authorities, for there is no authority except that which God has established. The authorities that exist have been established by God. Romans 13:1

Please write your responses to the following questions:

What are the three most important authority figures in your life that you are required to answer to? These don't have to be people. For example, you could list "the IRS" or "my school" if you wanted to.

1._____

_____

2._____

_____

3._____

_____

What is your relationship like with each of these people/entities and why is it the way it is?

1._____

_____

_____

2._____

_____

_____

3._____

_____

_____

What could each authority figure/ entity do to improve the relationship?

1._____

_____

_____

2._____

_____

_____

3._____

_____

_____

Describe some ways that you improve your relationship with these three authorities.

1._____

_____

_____

2._____
_____
_____

3._____
_____
_____

Are there any authority figures that you should be answering to but are ignoring?

_____
_____
_____
_____
_____
_____

How can your faith in God help you establish a better attitude and healthier relationships with those who are in authority over you?

_____
_____
_____
_____
_____
_____

Journal your thoughts about today's Scripture: <u>Scripture of the Day: Everyone must submit himself to the governing authorities, for there</u>

is no authority except that which God has established. The authorities that exist have been established by God. Romans 13:1
one.

_____
_____
_____
_____
_____
_____
_____

Can you submit and surrender yourself readily to authority, or do you constantly battle with rebellion, discomfort, unease, and anger? Let your answers today guide you into good relationships and positive behaviors that naturally flow from following God's plan for your life.

Today help me to give up control to you, the Maker and Creator of the world. Help me to understand that only heaven is perfect, and in this world the healthy option is to let you run my life. Lead me, direct me, love me, dear God.

Day Eighteen: Choosing to Give Authority to Others

Quote: Why consent to creep when you feel the urge to fly? -- Helen Keller

Mark's Introduction to the day: You can't fly unless you empower others to support you in flight. That means trusting others and giving them authority. An airplane may be flown by a pilot, but without a ground crew, flight operations, and maintenance, the plane becomes unsafe pretty quickly. Today we explore giving authority to others. This means giving up control and surrendering. Not easy to do! But no great team has a playbook for just one player. Who will you trust to be on your team?

Key Thought for the Day: In order to be truly successful in live, sometimes you have to give the authority to others.

Scripture of the Day: What, then, shall we say in response to this? If God is for us, who can be against us? (Romans 8:31)

Please write your responses to the following questions:

Let's start by taking some time to identify three people who have authority in your life by your choice:

1._____

2._____

3._____
_____
_____

How is your relationship with each of these people? Explain:
1._____
_____
_____

2._____
_____
_____

3._____
_____
_____

Are you satisfied with these relationships as they are? Why? Why not?
1._____
_____
_____

2._____
_____
_____

3._____
_____
_____

What emotions get in the way of these relationships (ex. Fear, anger, resentment, jealousy, etc)? Explain
1._____
_____
_____

2._____
_____
_____

3._____
_____
_____

What steps might you take to improve these relationships?
1._____
_____
_____

2._____
_____
_____

3._____
_____
_____

What are some ways that your authority figures could enable or empower you to improve your relationship with them?
1._____
_____
_____

2._____
_____
_____

3._____
_____
_____

Are there any one who should have a voice of authority in your life but doesn't? Explain

What can you do to change this?

Journal your thoughts about today's Scripture: *What, then, shall we say in response to this? If God is for us, who can be against us? (Romans 8:31)*

_____

_____

_____

Today I challenge you to think long and hard about the authority you've given to the people in your life. Remember the times that you've influenced others, and remember the times they have influenced you.

Dear God, you're the one authority that I need to be in relationship with daily. Help me get to know you better and love you more.

Day Nineteen: Giving in to the Authority to God's Word

Quote: "We may be certain that whatever God has made prominent in his Word he intended to be conspicuous in our lives." –Charles Spurgeon

Mark's Introduction to the day: So what is the most legitimate playbook that we can follow? Is it a story, song, novel, play? The Bible is God's playbook for our lives. Athletes will tell you that during the season they have to study the playbook and game plan daily. Studying the playbook allows us to get to know the plays, but also the playmaker as well. When we know God's design for us, we draw into a closer relationship with him and discover the benefits of His authority, love and affection.

Key Thought for the Day: God's Word Reveals His Will to Us.

Scripture of the Day: I have hidden your word in my heart that I might not sin against you. Psalm 119:1

Please write your responses to the following questions:

What does the word of God have to do with authority?

_____
_____
_____
_____
_____
_____
_____

Why is it important to allow God's Word to have authority in your life?
_____
_____
_____
_____
_____
_____
_____

Now let's list three times that you have willingly submitted yourself to the authority of God's word?

1._____
_____
_____

2._____
_____
_____

3._____
_____
_____

Describe how this decision affected your life in each case:

1._____
_____
_____

2._____
_____
_____

3._____
_____
_____

Now list three times when you did not answer to the authority of God's word:

1._____

_____

_____

2._____

_____

_____

3._____

_____

_____

Why is it sometimes difficult for you to submit yourself to the authority of God's Word?

_____

_____

_____

_____

_____

_____

_____

What are three ways that you can overcome this difficulty?

1._____

_____

_____

2._____

_____

_____

3._____

_____

_____

How can you use the authority of God's Word to benefit your relationship with the other authority figures in your life?

_____

_____

_____

_____

_____

_____

_____

How can you use the authority of God's Word to benefit your relationship with God?

_____

_____

_____

_____

_____

_____

_____

Journal your thoughts about today's Scripture: I have hidden your word in my heart that I might not sin against you. Psalm 119:1

_____

_____

_____

_____

_____

_____
_____
_____
_____
_____
_____
_____
_____
_____

God loves us and wants to keep us in his presence. To be in a close relationship with Him we need to submit to the Bible, God's Word, and its truth. How can we execute the plays that really matter if we don't know what God requires of us in the first place?

God, thank you for teaching me that authority is good and healthy when it comes from You. You've opened my eyes to your love. Help me to submit to you and your word daily so I can be with you forever.

Day Twenty: God is the Ultimate Authority. We must answer to Him first.

Quote: "Give yourself fully to God. He will use you to accomplish great things on the condition that you believe much more in His love than in your own weakness." – Mother Theresa

It has often been said, "If you don't believe in something, you will fall for anything." The concept of God as the ultimate authority can be difficult to accept. Each day we want, at the very least, to be in control and at the very most to be a like a god. Unfortunately, playing god doesn't work very well; loved ones get hurt, plans fail, and ultimately life ends. Being mature includes recognizing reality. And reality lets us know that we are not in control. Only, God, the Ultimate Authority is. Try today's questions on for size.

Key Thought for the Day: God is the ultimate authority.

Scripture of the Day: Trust in the LORD with all your heart and lean not on your own understanding; in all your ways acknowledge him, and he will make your paths straight. (Proverbs 3:5-6)

Please write your responses to the following questions:

Why is it so important for us all to put God first in our lives?

_____
_____
_____
_____
_____
_____

List three times when you consciously and intentionally put God first in your life?

1._____
_____
_____

2._____
_____
_____

3._____
_____
_____

How did these decisions affect your life?

1._____
_____
_____

2._____
_____
_____

3._____
_____
_____

How do you think things would have been different if you had not put God first?

_____
_____
_____
_____
_____

_____
_____

Now let's list three times that you did not put God first:
1._____
_____
_____

2._____
_____
_____

3._____
_____
_____

What affect did each of those decisions have on your life?
1._____
_____
_____

2._____
_____
_____

3._____
_____
_____

What might have turned out differently if you had put God first?
_____
_____
_____
_____
_____

_____
_____

What aspect of your life is most difficult for you to give over to God's authority? Why?

_____
_____
_____
_____
_____
_____

Suppose you handed over every aspect of your life to God? What is your worst fear?

_____
_____
_____
_____
_____
_____

What is your greatest hope?

_____
_____
_____
_____
_____
_____

Journal your thoughts about today's Scripture: *Trust in the LORD with all your heart and lean not on your own understanding; in all your ways acknowledge him, and he will make your paths straight. (Proverbs 3:5-6)*

_____
_____
_____
_____
_____
_____
_____
_____
_____
_____
_____
_____
_____
_____
_____
_____

I hope today's exercises helped you make some interesting discoveries about authority. I especially like to reflect on the outcome of times when God was first in my life, and the outcome of times when He wasn't. How can you put God first today?

Help me today to surrender to your wonderful authority, Lord, as you did with David. Let me be someone after your own heart because you are the God of authority and power. Teach me to follow you all the days of my life, help me to bend or even break for you.

Nurture:

In order to accomplish everything we've discussed, we must nurture our bodies and commit ourselves to what I call 'The Fabulous Five:' Fitness, Family, Faith, Finances, and Fellowship. Each of these elements has a role in helping us reach our ultimate goal—a more fulfilling life. And they are all important, because if just one is overlooked, all the others suffer. For the next five days, we'll focus on the Fabulous Five. And we will begin with one of my personal favorites: Fitness.

Day Twenty-one: Fitness

Quote: "You need to listen to your body because it sure listens to you. Your body speaks to you through your headaches, your painful back, your depression and your anxieties, even your constant colds. It informs you and confirms what you are saying to yourself." – Dr. Phil McGraw

We need to get in shape and stay in shape. But how can we do so in a world where we get older everyday, where our joints creak and our recovery time for activity keeps getting longer and longer? What is fitness? It is the ability to exercise our body, mind, spirit, and emotions regularly for the purpose of doing what God would have us do in an optimal way. Working out in all these areas creates flexibility, better recovery from stress, and a healthier attitude towards this world.

Key Thought for the Day: Let's take a look at the person that we want to become by first getting a handle on this body in which we make our home.

Scripture of the Day: Don't you know that you yourselves are God's temple and that God's spirit lives in you? (I Corinthians 3:16)

Please write your responses to the following questions:

Let's start by reviewing the four key types of fitness, mentioned in the introduction to this section. What are they? (If you can't remember, please review page --)

1._____
_____
_____

2._____
_____
_____

3._____

_____

4._____

_____

How are all of these aspects of fitness related? Why is being physically fit so important? What is the "triangle of power" and its significance?

For each of the four categories, describe two ways in which you have successfully maintained a level of fitness:

Physical

1._____

2._____

Mental

1._____

2._____
_____
_____

Emotional

1._____
_____
_____

2._____
_____
_____

Spiritual

1._____
_____
_____

2._____
_____
_____

How did seeking fitness in these four impact your life?

_____
_____
_____
_____
_____
_____

Now for each of the four categories, list two ways in which you could improve your level of fitness:

Physical
1._____
_____
_____

2._____
_____
_____

Mental
1._____
_____
_____

2._____
_____
_____

Emotional
1._____
_____
_____

2._____
_____
_____

Spiritual
1._____
_____
_____

2._____

Journal your thoughts about today's Scripture: *Don't you know that you yourselves are God's temple and that God's spirit lives in you? (I Corinthians 3:16)*

You take your body with you wherever you go. You also take your spirit, mind, and emotions into every encounter. The more fit you are, the more healthy those encounters and this life will be.

Father, help me change in my mind so that I can change in my body. Remove from me all those things that hold me back from healthiness in body, mind, emotions and spirit. God, please hear my prayer and create in me a disciplined lifestyle that allows me to draw nearer to you.

Day Twenty-two: Family

<u>Quote:</u> "Happiness is having a large, loving, caring, close knit family in another city." -- George Burns

One of the great pleasures and joys of my life was being in the YMCA's Indian Princess Program with my daughter, and the Indian Guide Program with my son. These programs are for dads and daughters/sons who are between 5 and 9 years old. The activities promote uninterrupted time together without cell phones, email, or the day to day distractions of the world. Through campouts and other learning experiences, about 10 dads and 10 kids get to enjoy adventure and each other's company.

I believe that we should try to practice uninterrupted time daily with our family and loved ones whenever possible. I hope you'll embrace the six purposes of the YMCA: Love the sacred circle of family, be clean in body and pure in heart, share understanding between parents and children, listen while others speak, love your neighbor as you love yourself, and see and preserve the beauty of God's work in the forest, field, and stream.

Key Thought for the Day: A family is a place where unconditional love, encouragement, and reaffirmation take place daily.

<u>Scripture of the Day:</u> <u>But if serving the LORD seems undesirable to you, then choose for yourselves this day whom you will serve…But as for me and my household, we will serve the LORD. (Joshua 24:15)</u>

Today rather than answering questions, let's meditate on the six purposes of the YMCA Indian princesses and come up with ways that we can effectively apply their wisdom to our lives!

Purpose # 1 – Love the sacred circle of family.

Why is this principle important to a healthy family?

_____
_____
_____
_____
_____
_____

List two ways that you can successfully apply this principle to your family's life:

1._____
_____
_____

2._____
_____
_____

Purpose #2 – Be clean in body and pure in heart.

Why is this principle important to a healthy family?

_____
_____
_____
_____
_____
_____

List two ways that you can successfully apply this principle to your family's life:

1._____
_____
_____

2._____
_____
_____

Purpose #3 – Share understanding between parents and children.

Why is this principle important to a healthy family?

_____
_____
_____
_____
_____
_____

List two ways that you can successfully apply this principle to your family's life:

1._____
_____
_____

2._____
_____
_____

Purpose #4 – Listen while others speak.

Why is this principle important to a healthy family?
_____
_____
_____
_____
_____
_____

List two ways that you can successfully apply this principle to your family's life:

1._____
_____
_____

2._____
_____
_____

Purpose #5 – Love your neighbor as you love yourself.

Why is this principle important to a healthy family?
_____
_____
_____
_____
_____
_____

List two ways that you can successfully apply this principle to your family's life:

1._____
_____
_____

2._____
_____
_____

Purpose #6 – See and preserve the beauty of God's work in the forest, field, and stream.

Why is this principle important to a healthy family?
_____
_____
_____
_____
_____
_____
_____

List two ways that you can successfully apply this principle to your family's life:

1._____
_____
_____

2._____
_____
_____

Journal your thoughts about today's Scripture: *But if serving the LORD seems undesirable to you, then choose for yourselves this day whom you will serve...But as for me and my household, we will serve the LORD. (Joshua 24:15)*

_____
_____
_____
_____
_____
_____
_____
_____
_____
_____
_____
_____
_____
_____

The battle for good relationships is won on the battleground of time. My wife and I stood side by side in church this week with our two beautiful children singing songs to our Creator. As we were singing I became overwhelmed by how great God is and how awesome our heavenly family will be. All of the negative things that we can experience here on earth will be gone. There will be no rejection or hurt, no abuse, and no abandonment or pain. God showed me what it can be like; a taste of the Godly family. I encourage you today to make your family a major priority. It is one of the only places where love is unconditional, encouragement is free, and the landing area is softer if we fall.

God, you know what a healthy family perspective and dynamic is. Please teach me the best way to have a godly relationship with each member of my family. Help me and my family to stay in union with you and to follow your word so that we can remain wholesome and spiritually healthy.

Day Twenty-three: Faith

Quote: "I have fought the good fight, I have finished the race, I have kept the faith." – Paul the Apostle

Faith - That which can't be qualified, but you sure know when it's missing! In Hebrews 11 we read that because of faith Abraham trusted God with his son Isaac. Because of faith the walls of Jericho fell. Because of faith David let God judge Saul. Because of faith we know that Christ died so that we can live. It is said that the best way to starve doubt is by feeding the faith through God's word.

Key Thought for the Day: Keep the faith!

Scripture of the Day: Without faith it is impossible to please God, because anyone who comes to him must believe that he exists and that he rewards those who earnestly seek him. (Hebrews 11:6)

Please answer the following questions:

Why is it important for you and for others to see your faith in action?
___
___
___
___
___
___
___

Is it hard for you to be faithful? Why or why not?
___
___

_____
_____
_____
_____
_____

Regardless of whether we're gifted with faith or not, we can always improve, right? Let's work through how to get this accomplished. First, what are three areas in your life in which you are required to have faith?

1._____
_____
_____

2._____
_____
_____

3._____
_____
_____

For each of your areas that you just listed, describe an event or events where your faith helped to enrich your life and/or the lives of others. How did this make you feel?

1._____
_____
_____

2._____
_____
_____

3._____
_____
_____

Now let's go back to the areas that you described in question three. For each of these areas, describe an event or events where you were not as faithful as you would have liked to be.

1._____

2._____

3._____

How might your lack of faith have affected the outcome of things?

_____
_____
_____
_____
_____
_____

Finally, what are three changes that you can make in yourself that will help you exercise your faith more effectively?

1._____

2._____

3._____
_____
_____

Journal your thoughts about today's Scripture: *Without faith it is impossible to please God, because anyone who comes to him must believe that he exists and that he rewards those who earnestly seek him. (Hebrews 11:6)*

_____
_____
_____
_____
_____
_____
_____
_____
_____
_____
_____
_____

Faith is a daily undertaking where we commit ourselves to be under God's direction and mercy in all of our endeavors. It's not easy to do! Faith takes practice—the practice of turning over control of our future to the Almighty.

Strengthen me, Lord, in my faith. Show me that by praying, worshiping, and serving you daily, my faith will flourish and I will see you more in the circumstances of my life. Mold me through faith to be more like you each day of my life.

Day Twenty-four: Finance

Quote: "Possessing material comforts in no way guarantees happiness. Only spiritual wealth can bring true happiness." – Konosuke Matsushita

Here's a song meant to be sung quickly and out of tune: "Budget, budget, budget that's all I ever hear. Budget, budget, budget! It's that time of year."

The Bible has over 3,000 references to finance and financial issues. The number two most referenced verses are on love at just over 700. That would suggest that finances are important. Even more important, however,, is understanding how we are supposed to deal with our finances. It's not about what I get and how wealthy I am -- it's all about what I do with whatever I have been given. Enjoy today's questions on wealth, money and finances and keep the perspective that you won't be here in a 100 years. See if that impacts any of your answers.

Key Thought for the Day: *If you had all the money you ever needed today, what would you do tomorrow?*

Scripture of the Day: "No one can serve two masters. Either he will hate the one and love the other, or he will be devoted to the one and despise the other. You cannot serve both God and money." (Matthew 6:24)

Please answer the following questions:

There's an old saying that goes, "you don't have money; money has you." What do you think this means?

_____
_____
_____
_____

_____
_____
_____

What does it mean to you to be "financially healthy?"
_____
_____
_____
_____
_____
_____
_____

Now let's come up with a plan to make the most of your finances no matter how abundant or lacking they may be. The first step is to take charge of your money. Let's come up with three ways to get in control of your money.

1._____
_____

2._____
_____

3._____
_____

For each of ideas you've just listed for taking charge of your finances, describe how you can make sure you follow through

1._____
_____
_____

2._____
_____
_____

3._____
_____
_____

Take a few moments to think about it, and then write what you believe to be the purpose of money. Then explain your thoughts.

_____
_____
_____
_____
_____
_____
_____

It has been said that a person's checkbook reveals more about his true intentions than his diary. Do you think you have a sense of purpose behind your financial decisions? Why? Why not?

_____
_____
_____
_____
_____
_____
_____

What are three changes that you can make in yourself that will help you possess a healthier and godlier sense of financial purpose?
1._____
_____
_____

2._____
_____
_____

3._____
_____
_____

Journal your thoughts about today's Scripture: *"No one can serve two masters. Either he will hate the one and love the other, or he will be devoted to the one and despise the other. You cannot serve both God and money."* (Matthew 6:24)

_____
_____
_____
_____
_____
_____
_____
_____
_____
_____
_____
_____

Zig Ziglar says, "I've got all the money I need for a house, but it won't buy me a home. All the money I need to buy affection, but it won't buy me love. All the money to buy a bed, but it won't buy me a good night's sleep." You see possessions, popularity, and pleasure are nice, but they are not profound and long-lasting. <u>Peace</u> of mind, <u>people</u> who I love and who love me, and <u>purpose</u> for my life must be developed through relationships.

Oh God, help me with the conflict and the burden of choosing between money and people. Help me develop the spirit, mind, and power to choose people over money every time. Let me know your love and let me share your love with others in ways that last.

Day Twenty-five: Fellowship

Quote: "Love each other or perish." – W.H. Auden

Fellowship - this is your community, your neighborhood, your town. Maybe you find fellowship in a charity or foundation, a church or synagogue you're associated with, or possibly some other type of group you identify with or volunteer your time to. Fellowship is where you live and how you impact others where you live. Today's questions will help develop a vision for your fellowship.

Key Thought for the Day: We cannot reach our full growth unless we support and help others!

Scripture of the Day: "For where two or three come together in my name, there am I with them." (Matthew 18:20)

Please answer the following questions:

What does the word "community" mean to you?

_____
_____
_____
_____
_____
_____
_____

What in your opinion is an ideal community?

_____
_____
_____

_____
_____
_____
_____

Are you part of a faith/fellowship community? Why or Why Not

_____
_____
_____
_____
_____
_____

If you aren't part of faith/fellowship community, what are some ways you could seek one?

_____
_____
_____
_____
_____
_____

If you are part of faith/fellowship community, do enjoy and find support in it? Why? Why not?

_____
_____
_____
_____

_____

_____

What are five ways that you can improve the community that you are in so that it is closer to your ideal community?

1._____

_____

_____

2._____

_____

_____

3._____

_____

_____

4._____

_____

_____

5._____

_____

_____

What are three things that you can do to become a better member of your fellowship community?

1._____

_____

_____

2._____

_____

_____

3._____

How can a strong fellowship with others help you with your fitness, family, faith, and finances?

Journal your thoughts about today's Scripture: *"For where two or three come together in my name, there am I with them." (Matthew 18:20)*

Fellowship and community are important. Ask any coach or teacher and they will tell you hands down that they get more out of the mentoring experience than the player or student does. Why? Because they are giving their gifts, talents, and experiences back to their community. Fellowship creates energy and accountability that allows the other four areas (fitness, family, faith, and finance) to work even better.

Show me the way to impact my community for you Lord. Teach me how to love, serve, and care for those that I meet outside of my family. Let me lead as Jesus did in the town and neighborhood you've put me in.

D = Direction

In Rick Warren's (no relation) book "The Purpose Driven Life," he builds on scripture to ask the question "What matters most?" The answer is Biblical -- love God and love others. How well we do this has determined the direction our life has gone, and will determine the direction we will go in the future. The last five plays in this book are about establishing direction, so be ready for some atypical goal setting and insight. It's not about your view of direction, your school or company's view, or the military's view. It's about all about God's direction. Over the course of these last days together let's work on drawing closer to God so that we can have the best possible understanding of his will in our lives.

Day Twenty-six: After thinking about your priorities for the past few days, now let's think about your life purpose.

Quote: "In the grand scheme of things, what matters is not how long you live, but why you live, what you stand for and are willing to die for." – Paul Watson

"Be still and know that I am God." I love this verse. It reminds me that all great action for God, all discernment of knowledge, starts with being still. Can you envision how being still could impact your decisions on focused direction and purpose? Take your time! This play takes a while to learn.

Key Thought for the Day: To have purpose is to know God

Scripture of the Day: "To everything there is a season, a time for every purpose under heaven." (Ecclesiastes 3:1 KJV)

Please answer the following questions:

How would you explain "having a life purpose" in your own words?

_____
_____
_____
_____
_____
_____
_____

Why is it important for each of us to identify our life purpose?
_____
_____
_____
_____
_____
_____
_____

Take a moment to think about the major facets of your life: your working life, family life, community life, and spiritual life.
Describe three ways that identifying your life purpose could improve your working life:
1._____
_____
_____

2._____
_____
_____

3._____
_____
_____

List three ways that identifying your life purpose could improve your family life:
1._____
_____
_____

2._____
_____
_____

3._____
_____
_____

List three ways that identifying your life purpose could improve your community life:

1._____
_____
_____

2._____
_____
_____

3._____
_____
_____

List three ways that identifying your life purpose could improve your spiritual life:

1._____
_____
_____

2._____
_____
_____

3._____
_____
_____

What is your life purpose?

_____
_____

Did you choose this purpose or do you feel like it was chosen for you? Explain.

Journal your thoughts about today's Scripture: *"To everything there is a season, a time for every purpose under heaven."* (Ecclesiastes 3:1 KJV)

I hope today's questions helped you identify your life purpose. Do you have increased clarity about your game plan? Any fresh ideas when it comes to direction? Enjoy the moment you are in! Be still and begin to discover God's plan for your life. But be prepared—it may be a little different than yours.

Lord show me the way. There are times when I have no clue, vision, or map. Help me trust you more each day. Let me step out in faith so that your direction for me will become evident. And Lord, if I need to wait, help me to wait patiently and to explore all the things you would have me consider. Most of all, please teach me to be still, and to know that you are God.

Day Twenty-seven: What do you hope to have accomplished a year from today?

Quote: If you don't know where you're going, any road will get you there." – Lewis Carroll

If one person trusts God and relies on Him, while another seeks only earthly gratification, there's bound to be a big difference in their ultimate outcomes. How do you quantify an eternal reward? If God had a conversation with you today, what might he say about focusing your hope and faith in him?

Key Thought for the Day: Quiet down and listen.

Scripture of the Day: "Now listen, you who say, 'Today or tomorrow we will go to this or that city, spend a year there, carry on business and make money.' Why, you do not even know what will happen tomorrow. What is your life? You are a mist that appears for a little while and then vanishes. Instead, you ought to say, 'If it is the Lord's will, we will live and do this or that.'" (James 4:13-15)

Please answer the following questions:

Today is all about setting goals yourself, and creating a plan that will allow you to successfully achieve these goals. Describe one instance from your past in which you set a goal for yourself and successfully attained it:

_____
_____
_____
_____
_____

_____
_____

How did achieving this goal affect your life?
_____
_____
_____
_____
_____
_____

How did achieving this goal make you feel?
_____
_____
_____
_____
_____
_____

Why is it important to set goals for yourself?
_____
_____
_____
_____
_____
_____

Now what about the future? Try to come up with five goals that you would like to have accomplished a year from now:

1._____

2._____

3._____

4._____

5._____

Briefly describe why you chose each goal:

1._____

2._____

3._____

4._____

5._____

Will you have to make any changes in your life in order to achieve these goals? Explain.

_____
_____
_____
_____
_____
_____

How do fit your faith into goal setting? Do you think God helps us in achieving our goals? How can we seek his help our quest?

_____
_____
_____
_____
_____
_____

Journal your thoughts about today's Scripture: *"Now listen, you who say, 'Today or tomorrow we will go to this or that city, spend a year there, carry on business and make money.' Why, you do not even know what will happen tomorrow. What is your life? You are a mist that appears for a little while and then vanishes. Instead, you ought to say, 'If it is the Lord's will, we will live and do this or that.'"* (James 4:13-15)

_____
_____
_____
_____
_____

_____
_____
_____
_____
_____
_____
_____

The five goals you've set can help you enjoy a life lived well over the next year. How will you stay with it and achieve those goals? Set up your own board of directors—friends and family members who will hold you accountable to God's standards and your five goals. They will become work-out partners, study partners, business partners, and marriage partners you can turn to.

Lord, only you know what the next year holds. Help me discern Your will and to focus my goals on loving You and loving others as you have loved me.

Day Twenty-eight: What do you hope to have accomplished five years from today?

Quote: "The true joy in life is being used for a purpose recognized by yourself as mighty, the being a force of nature." -- George Bernard Shaw

In five years what will your life look like? Will you have accomplished any of your goals? What relationships will have begun or ended? How old will you be? Each of us needs a process that allows God to lead and enables us to follow him. This means we need to become good listeners so we can hear what God is saying. We also need to be flexible and to have an optimistic perspective. That way, when God starts to move us, we will be ready, willing, and able to embark on the journey he has in mind.

Key Thought for the Day: Action today brings results tomorrow.

Scripture of the Day: "My times are in your hands." (Psalm 31:15)

Please answer the following questions:

Sometimes long term goals can seem like a waste of time. Why is it important for us to think about setting goals so far into the future?

_____
_____
_____
_____
_____
_____

Have you been successful in your past attempts at achieving long term goals? Why? Why not?

_____
_____
_____
_____
_____
_____
_____

Let's think about life without goals. Briefly describe three ways that your life would be different if you decided to never set any long term goals.

1._____
_____
_____

2._____
_____
_____

3._____
_____
_____

Let's get to the goal-setting. Take some time to come up with five goals that you would like to have accomplished within the next five years:

1._____
_____

2._____
_____

3._____
_____

4._____
_____

5._____
_____

Briefly describe why you chose each goal:

1._____
_____
_____

2._____
_____
_____

3._____
_____
_____

4._____
_____
_____

5._____
_____
_____

Will you have to make any changes in your life in order to achieve these goals? Explain.

_____
_____
_____
_____
_____
_____

How to you think God feels about our setting of long term goals? Explain.

Journal your thoughts about today's Scripture: *"My times are in your hands." (Psalm 31:15)*

God is ready to share his plan for your life with you if you will let him. God created you for a reason; you're not an accident. Whether you understand this truth today or not until five years from now, it's okay. God will have cared for you all along. Let him share the direction he has for you. Find him in the quiet and stillness of your life.

Father, help me to become more like Jesus. Teach me to follow your will for my life—not just for tomorrow but for next year, the next five years and into eternity. Help me to feel the needs of the lost and the hungry along the way, and to do my best to meet them. In Jesus name I pray.

Day Twenty-nine: Accepting Responsibility for Your Choices and Actions.

Quote: "We have gone from a society of responsibility and respect to a society of rights and privileges." -- Lou Holtz

Those who lead in life and accept responsibility for their choices and actions do so because they base their lives on universal principles and timeless truth. These are applied within the context of culture and society. God's principles give us tools and suggestions that drive our choices and actions. His word keeps us on the right path, and his spirit leads us along. His relationship with us through his son Jesus Christ allows us to evaluate our sinful state and to understand that we need his help in all we do.

Key Thought for the Day: We cannot reach our full growth unless—hard as it is—we accept responsibility for our choices and actions.

Scripture of the Day: "I can do everything through him who gives me strength." (Philippians 4:13)

Please answer the following questions:

Taking responsibility for our actions is usually not difficult when we are successful or have done something admirable. Why do you think is this true?

_____
_____
_____
_____

_____

_____

When things go wrong, however, taking responsibility for our actions can be very difficult. Taking responsibility usually means that we neither blame others nor see ourselves as victims. Try to list three times you were able to take responsibility for your actions, even though things went wrong:

1._____
_____
_____

2._____
_____
_____

3._____
_____
_____

Why was this easy or difficult for you? Explain.

_____
_____
_____
_____
_____
_____
_____

What effect did your taking responsibility have on the outcome of these circumstances?

_____
_____
_____

_____
_____
_____
_____

Now list three instances when you failed to accept responsibility for your actions.

1._____
_____
_____

2._____
_____
_____

3._____
_____
_____

Why was taking responsibility hard for you in those three instances?

_____
_____
_____
_____
_____
_____

What impact did your irresponsibility have on the outcome of these three situations?

_____
_____
_____
_____

Journal your thoughts about today's Scripture: "I can do everything through him who gives me strength." (Philippians 4:13)

Taking responsibility is a habit that grows out of discipline and desire to do what God commands. How can we find that discipline? We find it through the Word of God, through prayer, and through relationships with other believers.

Help me, Lord, to grow up and accept responsibility for my actions. Let my actions be guided by the Holy Spirit so that I am accountable to you as well as to those around me. I pray that the goodness you surround me with can be shared with others and that they'll see Jesus in all that I do and all that I am.

Day Thirty: Choose Significance Over Success.

Quote: "He who hath true and perfect charity, in no ways seeketh his own good, but desireth that God alone be altogether glorified." – Thomas a Kempis The Imitation of Christ

Mark's Introduction to the day: Wow, here we are at the end of the road with a topic as large as could ever be. Significance or success - one is worldly, the other is eternal. Success in the world comes in many shapes and sizes. Significance, on the other hand, takes on very specific characteristics. These are qualities such as loving God with all your heart and making sure that he comes first in everything, and loving your neighbor and serving him or her as Jesus would. Today, let's identify the differences between success and significance, and spend some time discovering the truth about each one.

Key Thought for the Day: Choose significance over success!

Scripture of the Day: "I am the vine; you are the branches. If a man remains in me and I in him, he will bear much fruit; apart from me you can do nothing." (John 15:5)

Please answer the following questions:

What does it mean to you to live a successful life?

_____
_____
_____
_____
_____
_____
_____

Why is it important to be successful?

_____
_____
_____
_____
_____
_____
_____

Success isn't a bad thing! However, it can become a problem. Let's brainstorm five ways that success can become a problem.

1._____
_____
_____

2._____
_____
_____

3._____
_____

4._____
_____
_____

5._____
_____
_____

What does "significance" mean to you?

_____
_____
_____

What does it mean to you to live a significant life?

Do you believe that you are choosing to live a significant life right now? Why? Why not?

Explain what you think it means to "choose significance over success"?

Can you think of a time when you set success aside and chose significance instead? Explain.

_____
_____
_____
_____
_____
_____
_____

What are three areas of your life in which you need to focus more on significance than success?

1._____
_____
_____

2._____
_____
_____

3._____
_____
_____

How could setting aside success and pursuing significance improve your relationship with others?

_____
_____
_____
_____
_____
_____
_____

How could seeking significance in your life instead of success improve you relationship with God?

___

Journal your thoughts about today's Scripture: *I am the vine; you are the branches. If a man remains in me and I in him, he will bear much fruit; apart from me you can do nothing."* (John 15:5)

___

What have you learned about significance vs. success? Significance is making my life count. It is about people, peace of mind, and purpose. Success is about possessions, pleasures, and popularity. Significance is relationship oriented and success is more thing or material related. Which way have you chosen?

Thank you Lord God for giving me a chance to understand and explore significance and success. Let me chose significance. I am here to serve you and I love you. Lord, please help me make my life count for your purpose.

The Final Wrap-Up

Over the last 30 days, by working through this playbook, you have explored your dreams, passions, desires, and goals. And you've created your own personal game plan for living a more fulfilling life. So now, what do you do with it? Does it become like the business plan that goes in a drawer in your desk and never comes out again? Or do you make the effort and put it into action?

Please take the time to share your playbook with someone you trust. Get some feedback; try to eliminate a blind spot or two. Then begin to pursue the life that God has planned for you. Nothing in this world can take the place of knowing your life's purpose. Don't let the influence of society, culture, or religious dogma slow you down or impede your self-discovery. There are too many people in this world who are doing the wrong things and wasting the gifts, experiences, heart, and tools they were given.

Above all else remember: fulfillment and purpose are achieved by loving God and helping others. This is our life mission. With a little help from the ones you love the most, and a lot of help from God, I hope you'll put everything you've learned to good use in the days, months and years ahead.